SHIRE GARDEN H

D0260125

Public Parks

Hazel Conway

Corporation Park, Blackburn, c.1877.

Published in 1996 by Shire Publications Ltd, Cromwell House, Church Street, Princes Risborough, Buckinghamshire HP27 9AA, UK.
Copyright © 1996 by Hazel Conway. First published 1996. Number 9 in the Shire Garden History series. ISBN 0 7478 0332 3.
Hazel Conway is hereby identified as the author of this work in accordance with Section 77 of the Copyright, Designs and Patents Act 1988.

Printed in Great Britain by CIT Printing Services, Press Buildings, Merlins Bridge, Haverfordwest, Pembrokeshire SA61 1XF.

British Library Cataloguing in Publication Data: Conway, Hazel. Public Parks. – (Shire garden history; no. 9). 1. Parks – Great Britain – History. 2. Title. 712.5'0941. ISBN 0-7478-0332-3.

ACKNOWLEDGEMENTS

So many people have helped me in my exploration of parks over the past two decades that it is impossible to mention them all by name. I would, however, particularly like to thank all the local history librarians who have been so generous with their time and Alan Barber, Christopher Dingwall, Patrick Eyres, Keith Goodway, Stewart Harding, Fiona Jamieson, Harriet Jordan, David Lambert, Rowan Roenisch, Janet Storrie and Sandy Tosh.

Photographs are reproduced by courtesy of the following: Alan Barber, page 78; the British Architectural Library, pages 18-19; Christopher Dingwall, pages 17, 42 (top) and 47 (bottom); Patrick Eyres, page 69; Glasgow Museums: The People's Palace, pages 58 and 61; Keith Goodway, pages 70 and 74; Greater London Record Office, pages 54 and 79; Stewart Harding, page 75 (top); David Lambert, page 71 (top); Liverpool Libraries and Information Services, pages 14 and 40; Nottinghamshire County Council, Leisure Services, page 62; Janet Storrie, page 38; Sandy Tosh, page 51 (bottom).

Front cover: *The bandstand in Queen's Park, Crewe, 1887.*

Contents

Medal commemorating Queen Victoria's Diamond Jubilee and the opening of Hanley Park, Stoke-on-Trent, 1897.

Introduction

Public parks are familiar to most people today either because we make use of them in our daily lives or because we played in them as children. Every town of any size has its public parks, gardens and recreation grounds and we tend to take for granted that they will always be there, available for us to use freely. They were created throughout Britain during the nineteenth century and the first decades of the twentieth century, initially as part of the response to the appalling problems of the urban environment brought about by industrialisation and rapid population growth.

The term 'public park' implies a park that is fully and freely open to the public and London's royal parks are perhaps the best-known examples in Britain. One of the most influential royal parks of the early nineteenth century was Regent's Park, which was designed between 1811 and 1826 by John Nash, favourite architect of the Prince Regent (later George IV). Regent's Park only gradually became accessible to the public, for the royal parks were not always as fully open to the public as they are today. Richmond Park, for example, was enclosed with a high wall by Charles I, thereby shutting out several parishes that had rights of common, as well as blocking public footpaths. It did not become fully open to the public until 1904. Hyde Park opened to the public in the 1630s, but in 1705 Queen Anne appropriated 100 acres (40 hectares) in order to make an enclosure for deer and antelope. St James's Park had been formed by Charles II, but Queen Caroline, George II's consort, considered shutting the public out of the park and asked Sir Robert Walpole what it would cost to do so. 'Only a crown, madam,' was his reply.

The public parks that are the subject of this book are distinct from royal parks for they are municipal parks owned by local authorities. Britain was at the forefront of the industrial revolution and was the first country to establish municipal parks. Until the 1980s and 1990s it was only in municipal parks that the inalienable right of free public access was secure.

As the population of Britain increased and towns expanded in the late eighteenth and early nineteenth centuries new buildings spread over the open spaces in and around the towns and cities. In the mid eighteenth century the population of England and Wales was six million and only one person in five lived in a town of any size. A century later the census of 1851 showed that the population had risen to eighteen million and was divided equally between town and country dwellers. By the census of 1911 the population had again doubled and by that date 80 per cent of the people lived in towns. Industrial cities such as Manchester, Liverpool, Leeds and Birmingham are generally thought of as being the focus of this population explosion, but resorts such as Brighton, Blackpool and Southend-on-Sea were growing at an even greater rate.

In the early decades of the nineteenth century the problems resulting from massive unplanned urban expansion began increasingly to be recognised. The Utilitarians following the social ideals of Jeremy Bentham and John Stuart Mill stressed the need for action in order to bring about the 'greatest happiness for the greatest number'. Others remembered the French Revolution and were aware of growing working-class movements such as Chartism. Their concern for the welfare of the poorest members of urban society was motivated less by social ideals and more by fears of revolution, threats to security and the preservation of property rights.

As the towns continued to expand, the opportunities for recreation in green surroundings dwindled. Official recognition of this problem dates from 1833 when the Select Committee on Public Walks presented its report to Parliament. This report surveyed the accessible open space in the major towns and cities of England and showed how greatly parks were needed physically, socially and politically and the benefits that they could bring. London was the only city with parks – the royal parks, but there were none in the East End or south of the Thames. The park promoters thought that parks would provide fresh air and places for city dwellers to take exercise and so improve the physical health of the people. They would provide contact with nature and an alternative form of recreation to the tavern and so they would provide a civilising influence on those urban citizens most thought to be in need of improvement. They would provide a location where members of the different classes could meet and learn from each other and this would help to reduce social tensions. In addition, the creation of parks would provide opportunities for financial investment if, as at Regent's Park, they were developed together with new housing.

Until towns had grown considerably there was little need to set aside space especially for recreation, for the open land in and around them was still accessible. Expanding towns brought with them increases in land values. Commons, the traditional places for recreation, were enclosed, but the commoners received no compensation, nor did those who had lost their traditional places of recreation.

The law locks up the man or woman
Who steals the goose from off the Common
But lets the greater robber loose
Who steals the Common from the goose.

All sorts of events took place on commons, such as fairs, election meetings and a variety of sports. Kennington Common in London became the place where the growing working-class movements assembled and political meetings were held. The most famous of these was held on 14th April 1848, when some 25,000 supporters of the National Charter met there to carry their petition to Parliament. The Select Committee on Public Walks (SCPW) had suggested in 1833 that Kennington Common should become a public park. This idea was revived in 1851 and Kennington Park opened the following year.

While the commons in and around the expanding towns were being enclosed urban spaces such as squares, cemeteries and churchyards remained. The squares provided open space and were pleasant to see from the street, but they were generally not accessible to the public for only the residents of the houses around the squares, the keyholders, had access to them.

Churchyards and cemeteries were freely open to all, as were the few public walks that had been laid out in the eighteenth century. The Quarry in Shrewsbury was laid out along the banks of the Severn and in Dorchester the ruins of the Roman fortifications had been laid out with trees and walks in the early eighteenth century. In Leicester the 9 metres wide New Walk laid out by the local authority in 1785 led from the city centre to the countryside and later the racecourse. Today it runs from the city centre to Victoria Park, which was created on the site of the racecourse in 1880.

In the early years of the nineteenth century zoological and botanic gardens opened in increasing numbers. Entry to these was either by payment of a fee or by membership subscription, so they were not freely accessible. Pleasure gardens were another form of urban open space and although entry to them was not free they tended to draw their patrons from a broader cross-section of society than the zoological and botanic gardens. Pleasure gardens provided walks and gardens, music, drinking, dancing, theatre, masquerades, balloon ascents and fireworks. As the century progressed many of them faced fierce competition. Land values were increasing and moral attitudes changed. Pleasure gardens gained a reputation as a meeting place for pickpockets, prostitutes and drunkards and they began to be closed down. Vauxhall Gardens, the most famous of the London pleasure gardens, closed in 1859 and the site was let for building. The SCPW Report noted that the provision of parks would lead to a better use of Sundays and the replacement of 'the debasing pleasures now in vogue' by 'innocent amusements'. There were good reasons for these so-called 'debasing pleasures' for in most towns all the accessible open spaces were closed on Sunday, the one day in the week that people had time for recreation. An iron merchant told the Select Committee on Drunkenness (1834) that on Sunday in Liverpool 'all the public houses are open and all the public walks, cemeteries, zoological gardens and botanical gardens, where people might amuse themselves innocently, are closed'. Liverpool was not exceptional, for this tended to be the pattern throughout Britain.

As the park movement gathered momentum through the nineteenth century and into the twentieth, so the ideals of the park promoters were reflected in their design, in their planting, in the buildings and statues in them and in the activities that were permitted or forbidden in them. In a sense these parks represented ideal landscapes, separated from the realities of their urban surroundings, in which the air was clean and where the spirit could be refreshed by contact with nature and the body improved by exercise. They were at the same time practical, physical landscapes set in urban environments and they reflected the social, economic and political imperatives of the time.

The creation of these people's parks for the use of all urban citizens began at a time when there was no town planning and the structure of local government was only just evolving. When local authorities eventually gained the powers to make the urgently needed urban improvements, they were justifiably proud. No one was more vocal than Joseph Chamberlain in his civic crusade for Birmingham and in his belief in 'the organised power of a great representative assembly' that was Birmingham's local government. Parks became civic status symbols, as was clear to John Barran, the Mayor of Leeds. He argued that if the Council acquired Roundhay Park 'it would be as great a credit to them as their town hall [and]...give them a status in a way that few things would'.

By the end of the nineteenth century public parks had become an essential part of the urban fabric and as much part of the effort to raise living standards as libraries, art galleries and museums. Then the word 'municipal' was synonymous with pride in local powers and their ability to effect positive change. Local authorities could invest in parks and were proud to do so. Today the word has a pejorative ring which is almost the antithesis of its former meaning.

Local authorities no longer have the powers or the funding to create or maintain parks, but they still have the responsibility for their maintenance. In the nineteenth century there was little time and few opportunities for recreation. Now there is a wide variety of opportunities and some people are wondering if urban parks are still needed and, if they are, whether so many are required.

This history of public parks traces their development and the influences that lay behind their design. It looks at the features that give each park its individual character: the landscape, the trees, the lakes, the buildings such as lodges, shelters, bandstands and palm houses, the statues and the planting. It considers the changing attitudes to parks and why they have become neglected in the 1980s and 1990s and it looks at the role of parks in cities today and in the future.

The early public parks and Joseph Paxton

The park movement grew gradually during the 1830s and 1840s as initiatives were taken by central and local government, by benefactors, entrepreneurs and communities. The first park to be called Victoria Park was developed in Bath and opened by the young Princess Victoria in 1830. The Royal Victoria Park was a public park but it was not a municipal park as the land was leased and not owned by the local authority. In London the second Victoria Park was created in the East End, Primrose Hill near Regent's Park was secured as a public open space, and Parliament took the first steps towards forming Battersea Park.

The main thrust of park development, however, occurred in the major industrial towns of the north-west of England and in Glasgow. The first of the new industrial towns to create a municipal park was Preston, where the council enclosed the Town Moor in order to improve it and make it more beneficial to the community. Moor Park opened in 1833 and therefore qualifies as the first of the 'modern' nineteenth-century municipal parks. Unlike other enclosures, this one was undertaken by the borough council, who argued that as the Moor was used only by the burgesses and was not common land there was no need for an Act of Parliament to enclose it. At that date Preston Moor was partially laid out with a serpentine lake, lodges at the east and west entrances and walks. It was later fully laid out by Edward Milner in 1864.

Benefactors came forward with gifts of parks. One of these gifts, Derby Arboretum, was designed by John Claudius Loudon, who was one of the most important early designers of public parks. Manchester became the first of the major industrial cities to acquire public parks. In Liverpool the successful financial lessons of park development in conjunction with housing, seen first at Regent's Park in London, were applied by a speculator in Prince's Park. Across the Mersey similar principles were applied by the local authority in Birkenhead. These two ventures gave Joseph Paxton his first opportunities to design public parks.

Parks were developed on a variety of sites. These included the gardens of substantial mansions; the commons and greens that were already playgrounds and meeting places for the people; quarries, marshland, infill sites and other land unsuitable for building. Since there was as yet no national policy, their creation tended to be piecemeal and many different ways were found to create them.

The opening of a park was a cause for great celebration. When Derby Arboretum opened in 1840 there were three days of celebration with processions, balloon ascents, fireworks and events for children. When Birkenhead Park opened seven years later ten thousand people gathered to enjoy the bands, the bellringers and especially the rural sports. These included sack races, porridge-eating races and catching the greasy pig, which had been specially shaved, its tail soaped in readiness for this ordeal.

The main influences on the design of the early public parks came from the late eighteenth- and early nineteenth-century landscaping of Humphry Repton and John Nash and the work of John Claudius Loudon. It was Repton who first set down the principles of landscape gardening and identified the sources of pleasure in it. Curiosity was stimulated by novelty and variety and by picturesque beauty. This meant that there should be elements of surprise and that not all the features of a park should be visible at once. Appropriation meant enhancing the apparent extent of a site and to do this the boundaries or the exits should not be immediately visible. Animation, such as the movement caused by the wind rippling water or by animals grazing, enlivened the scene. Nash applied these principles at Regent's Park, as many later public park designers did elsewhere. Regent's Park was particularly influential on the design of public parks, not only because it was a royal park in London, designed by Nash, but also because of the way in which it had been created together with housing in and around it. The park added value to the properties and the sale of the housing helped to pay for the building of the park. This indeed was the thinking that lay behind the development of Victoria Park in east London.

The creation of a park to serve the East End of London had been one of the recommendations of the Select Committee on Public Walks. Towards the end of the 1830s a series of public meetings was held in the East End and as a result a petition of thirty thousand signatures was presented to the Queen in 1840 stressing the high mortality rate of the district, the appalling living conditions and the need for a park. After the necessary legislation had been passed Victoria Park was laid out by James Pennethorne, who had worked with John Nash on Regent's Park. Victoria Park provides an early illustration of some of the problems of park creation. A number of sites were investigated and Pennethorne's preference was for a site to the south which was nearer the population centre of the area. However, this was more expensive and the Bonner's Field site to the north was chosen instead. Like Regent's Park, the plan was for

The opening of Birkenhead Park, 1847.

a park with housing around but, unlike Regent's Park, the plots did not sell. Because only limited funds were available for the development of Victoria Park, the roads intended to link it to the City were not built and consequently the project proved unattractive to investors.

Victoria Park opened for use in 1845 although its design was still incomplete. The following year two lakes were excavated and a pagoda from Hyde Park Corner was moved to an island on the western lake. An arboretum was planted so that visitors could not only enjoy the variety of trees but also learn about them. The site was completely flat and in the 1850s, when John Gibson, who had trained with Paxton, was in charge of the park, plans were put forward for contouring it, but funds were insufficient to allow this. The design of Victoria Park evolved over a number of years and according to the *Illustrated London News* of 1873 it was by that date the real people's park for Londoners because of its varied features and design.

After the two early Victoria Parks, it was not until the end of the century that 'Victoria' again became a popular name for parks, although a number of parks were named 'Queen's Park' during the intervening years. It was the commemoration of Queen Victoria's Golden Jubilee in 1887, her Diamond Jubilee in 1897 and finally

her death in 1901 that led to the creation of an enormous number
of Victoria Parks throughout Britain.

Another important early park was Derby Arboretum, which opened
in 1840. Derby was growing fast and there were no commons or
wasteland nearby for recreation, so the textile manufacturer Joseph
Strutt decided to remedy the situation by donating a park to the
town. The designer he chose was the foremost landscape gardener
of the time, John Claudius Loudon. Loudon's influence came from
his prolific writings, and as editor of the *Gardeners' Magazine*,
the *Magazine of Natural History* and the *Architectural Magazine*
he had the outlets to express his ideas. Loudon had been taught by
Jeremy Bentham and was concerned with many important social
issues such as education, town planning, working-class housing
and clean air. In 1822 he began writing about the need for public
open space in his *Encyclopaedia of Gardening* and this was followed
by designs for the Birmingham Botanic Garden in 1831 and the
design of his first public park, the Terrace Garden, on a small 1.5
hectare site in Gravesend, in 1836. (This no longer exists.) Derby
Arboretum was three times larger than this, so Loudon had greater
scope for putting his social and landscape ideals into practice. Indeed,
he considered Derby Arboretum to be the most important commission
of his career.

Loudon's problem was to preserve the existing garden, minimise
maintenance costs and design a park which would not become boring
after a few visits. Variety in the landscaping and planting was needed,
but a botanic garden would be expensive to maintain. An arboretum
with a collection of native and non-native trees and shrubs, each
labelled with its name, history, uses and country of origin would,
he thought, provide beauty, variety, interest and education the whole
year round. More than eight hundred species were planted on
undulating mounds of soil so that the individual character and beauty
of each specimen could be appreciated. This was the principle of
the 'gardenesque' style of planting, which had first been proposed
by Loudon in his *Gardeners' Magazine* of December 1832. It allowed
each plant to develop its natural form as completely as possible,
uncrowded by its neighbours. As the Arboretum would soon be
surrounded by the expanding town of Derby, Loudon's design focused
all the interest within the site. Undulating mounds concealed the
boundaries of the park, as well as screening people who were walking
on adjacent paths from each other, so creating the illusion that the
Arboretum was larger than it really was. Loudon's design combined
axial symmetry of the straight paths with informal serpentine paths
around the edge of the site. Classical pavilions provided seats and

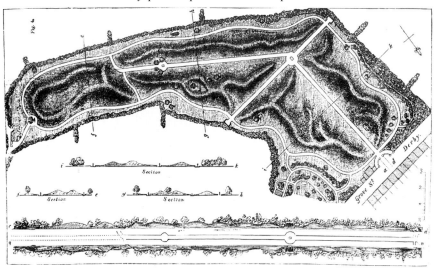

Plan of Derby Arboretum showing the undulating ground.

shelter at either end of the cross-walk, while at the junction of the main walks was a statue on a pedestal. At the entrances were picturesque Tudor and Elizabethan lodges with steeply pitched roofs and tall chimneys. These included refreshment rooms where visitors could eat their sandwiches, and toilets were available nearby.

The gift of Derby Arboretum created problems for the local authority, for at that date they were not allowed to use the rates to maintain it. Funds for its maintenance were raised by subscriptions and entry fees, but since Strutt's gift was intended for all the people of Derby free entry was allowed on part of Sunday and on Wednesdays from dawn to dusk. It was not until 1882 that there was completely free access.

The first of the major industrial cities to acquire parks was Manchester. Funds for three parks were raised by subscription from the local community; although the project was backed by individual councillors, the local authority made no financial contribution. Philips Park and Queen's Park in Manchester and Peel Park in Salford opened in 1846. After the official opening the parks were handed over to their respective local authorities. To commemorate this occasion, a notice at Philips Park proclaimed: 'This park was purchased by the people, was made for the people and is given to the people for their protection.'

Public park design involved very different problems from those encountered in the design of private parks and designers had to provide varied landscapes and a range of facilities, often within

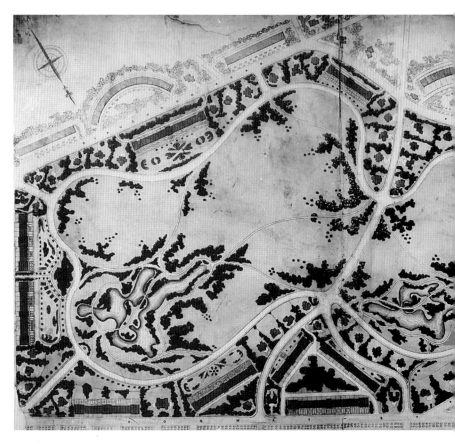

very restricted budgets. They also had to accommodate very large numbers of people, while at the same time preserving a feeling of space and contact with nature. The competition for the Manchester and Salford parks stressed the need for a variety of facilities and that the parks were for the public, not private use. Joshua Major was the winner and his designs featured open areas of grass for sports and for large numbers of people to gather, as well as flower gardens and rose gardens where people could stroll or sit in peace. Around the edges of the sites he placed various facilities for recreation, which included shuttlecocks, quoits, skittles, skipping, swings, gymnasia and archery. These were screened from each other by trees and shrubs to separate the various activities and to provide a measure of privacy.

Plan of Birkenhead Park, c.1845.

Joseph Paxton and his influence

The leading designers of private parks also worked on public parks and after Loudon's death in 1843 the most important was undoubtedly Joseph Paxton, not only because of the many parks that he designed in England and Scotland, but also because of his influence on those who trained with him. Paxton's career as gardener, architect and engineer is the archetypal Victorian success story and his reputation as head gardener to the sixth Duke of Devonshire at Chatsworth was well established by the time he came to design his first public park. This was the speculative development in 1842 of Prince's Park, Liverpool, which combined a park with housing around it, as at Regent's Park. Prince's Park was intended for the use of the residents only and was simply laid out with grass, stands of trees and a lake in one corner. It eventually became a municipal park in 1908. Across the river Mersey, the Birkenhead Improvement Commissioners were also considering developing a park and they too looked to Paxton. In 1842 the Commissioners promoted a private Bill to borrow funds to create a park with housing around it on some marshy land, and repay the loan out of the rates. Between 1842 and 1845, while the Bill was going through Parliament, the value of the land increased sevenfold and several members of the Commission who had speculated in this land benefited handsomely from the increase. Birkenhead was the first town to apply to Parliament for powers to use public funds to create a municipal park and for this reason Birkenhead Park has been credited as being the first municipal park. The park opened to the public in 1847. However, the first local authority to take action to create a municipal park was Preston and Moor Park (1833) would therefore appear to be the first municipal park.

The site for Birkenhead Park was divided by a main road and the land needed to be drained before it could be laid out. The plan shows the proposed terraces of housing and some formal planting around the edge of the park, while the interior offers expanses of open grass, with vistas across the whole park. In each part of the park is a lake, which assisted with the drainage of the site. The lakes have small islands in them, so the whole expanse of water could not be seen at one glance and the size of the lakes is not immediately apparent. The lake edges are well planted and footpaths wind around them offering a variety of views. Paxton wished to create a variety of landscapes and since the site was flat he raised mounds around the lakes, using the spoil from the lakes, created dramatic rocky outcrops and planted them with trees. These mounds and rocks enclose the areas around the lakes, frame views of the contrasting open parkland and add variety and contrast to the landscape. Paxton's plan gave no indication of the location of any sports facilities and these were subsequently accommodated as requests were made, unlike Joshua Major's plans for the Manchester and Salford parks, where provision was made from the outset. At Birkenhead Park Paxton introduced a very sophisticated circulation system. Near the boundary of the park is a serpentine route for

Rocky outcrops around the lake in Birkenhead Park.

Kelvingrove Park, Glasgow, c.1900.

carriages and horse riders to drive or ride in the park and there is a separate system of paths for pedestrians. F. L. Olmsted, an American landscape gardener, visited Birkenhead Park twice, in 1850 and in 1859, and wrote vividly of the features that he found there. Inspired by what he had seen, he developed many of these ideas when he came to design Central Park, New York, with Calvert Vaux.

After the successful completion of Prince's Park and Birkenhead Park Paxton went on to design two parks in Glasgow, Kelvingrove Park (1854) and Queen's Park (1862), both developed in conjunction with housing. These were followed by the Crystal Palace Park in Sydenham near London (1856), People's Park in Halifax (1857) and two more parks in Scotland, Baxter Park, Dundee (1863), and his last design before he died in 1865, the Public Park in Dunfermline (1866).

Of all these designs, the one that proved the most influential was Crystal Palace Park. The Crystal Palace, designed by Paxton for the Great Exhibition in Hyde Park in 1851, was moved in 1852 to a new site at Sydenham purchased by Paxton and the directors of the Crystal Palace Company. The intention was a speculative venture to create a new type of pleasure garden, which, unlike the existing pleasure gardens, would offer 'refined recreation to elevate the intellect and instruct the mind' in all weathers. The enlarged new

Bird's eye view of the Crystal Palace at Sydenham, 1854.

Crystal Palace was sited at the top of a hill and, to provide an appropriate setting, Paxton introduced Italian baroque principles of garden design. A series of grand terraces featured fountains, cascades and water temples and massed bedding plants on an unprecedented scale. The terraces provided a platform for viewing the surroundings, a place to display the water features and statuary and a focus for festivities. From them the layout of the park was visible below, while in the distance were wonderful views of the North Downs. A portrait head of Paxton was erected in 1869 and still stands in Crystal Palace Park. Beyond the terraces and to the side of them the landscape became more informal while at the further end of the park there was a lake with islands, similar to those in Paxton's earlier parks. Instead of providing a haven for ducks and other water birds these islands were inhabited by a collection of life-sized replicas of prehistoric animals.

Paxton's introduction of the formal element of the terrace became a characteristic of his parks, and some of the parks by designers who trained with Paxton also show similar formal features. In the People's Park, Halifax (1857), Paxton introduced a terrace, but on a much smaller scale, providing views over the park to the moors beyond, while pavilions in the form of an Italian loggia gave shelter from the rain. In the central pavilion was a large seated statue of the donor of the park, Sir Francis Crossley. Terraces had a practical purpose, for the raised surface dried quickly, enabling visitors to walk along them when the paths under the trees were still dripping. On the opposite side of the park from the terrace were small lakes, as at Crystal Palace Park, but scaled down so as to be in proportion with the rest of People's Park. To prevent the surroundings intruding on the park, Paxton, like Loudon, raised mounds around the boundary and screened the entrances with rocky outcrops

People's Park, Halifax, 1857.

so that the park proper was not immediately visible on entering.

Paxton's influence was continued by those who trained with him and then went on to design public parks themselves. Amongst them were Edward Milner, John Gibson and Edward Kemp, each of whom made substantial contributions to the design of public parks. Milner worked with Paxton on Prince's Park, Crystal Palace Park and the People's Park, Halifax. He then set up his own practice and designed three parks in Preston, parks in Glossop and Buxton, Lincoln Arboretum (1872) and the garden of St Paul's Cathedral, London (1879). He also became director of the Crystal Palace School of Gardening.

John Gibson became superintendent of Victoria Park in London in 1849 and then worked with Pennethorne on the design of Battersea Park (1856), where he established an international reputation for his introduction of the subtropical garden. In 1871 he became overseer of London's royal parks and two years later he designed Cannon Hill Park in Birmingham.

Kemp worked with Paxton at Birkenhead Park and became its first head gardener. He subsequently went on to design Grosvenor Park in Chester (1867), Hesketh Park in Southport (1868), Saltwell Park in Gateshead (1877) and Stanley Park in Liverpool (1870). Grosvenor Park lies along the river Dee and on its slopes Kemp created a rockery with rushing cascades and tranquil pools. This was overlooked by bastions which provided seating and viewing points over the rockery and river. Above, at the crossing of two straight footpaths lined by magnificent clipped glossy dark-green hollies, stands the statue of the park's donor, the Duke of Westminster.

Right: *The Duke of Westminster, the donor of Grosvenor Park, Chester.*

Below: *Holly walk, Grosvenor Park, Chester.*

Later Victorian parks

From the early days of the park movement benefactors had come forward to donate parks to local authorities but at the end of the 1850s the role of the benefactor was stimulated by two Acts of Parliament. As a result there was an increase in the donation of parks in the 1860s and 1870s. Despite this encouragement of benefactors and the difficulties inhibiting local authorities at this time, many more parks were developed by local authorities than by donors in every decade of the nineteenth century. Donors included aristocrats, local dignitaries, landowners and entrepreneurs. The Norfolks of Sheffield, the Calthorpes of Birmingham and the Seftons of Liverpool all donated parks that perpetuated their names, as did the entrepreneur Alexander Kay in Kilmarnock, Titus Salt, the alpaca manufacturer, in Saltaire, West Yorkshire, and many others.

The benefactor's role could be purely philanthropic, or it could include a measure of self-interest. In general that self-interest was best served by the donor retaining an interest in the land around the park for the development of housing. However, as at Victoria Park in London, such projects were not invariably successful, as Z. C. Pearson, the donor of Pearson Park and twice Mayor of Hull, discovered. Pearson retained sites on three sides of the park for building, but the project ran into financial difficulties. The park, designed by J. C. Niven, opened in 1860 but at that time Pearson's affairs were under investigation and he was unable to attend.

Niven trained with Paxton but his work shows little of Paxton's influence and at Pearson Park he planted trees to frame views across the landscape. In Fountain Gardens, Paisley (1868), Niven adopted a geometric plan with a magnificent cast-iron ornamental fountain at the centre, manufactured by George Smith & Sons of Glasgow. Both the fountain and the park were the gift of Thomas Coats. In the park stands a statue of Robert Burns, erected from the proceeds of the Tannahill Choir, 1884-95. Under the care of Niven the Hull parks became known for their wild-flower collections and indeed became the model for later public parks. In Hull's Botanic Garden he planted giant hogweed (*Heracleum mantegazzianum*), restricting its invasive tendencies by planting it on an island.

Other significant events during the 1860s increased the pressure for parks. A direct stimulus for park development in Lancashire came from the cotton famine. Lancashire depended on the United

Miller Park, Preston, c.1900.

States for 80 per cent of its raw cotton and when the southern ports were blockaded as a result of the American Civil War unemployment rocketed. Various acts were passed to provide relief to the areas worst affected and local authorities were allowed to borrow money for public works, including work on parks. At Blackburn Corporation Park was improved and a carriage drive to the top of the hill was constructed by unemployed cotton workers. Oldham bought the site for Alexandra Park and this opened in 1868. In Preston the council asked Edward Milner to design Avenham, Miller and Moor Parks. Unemployed cotton workers levelled and made the roads in all three parks. Miller Park and Avenham Park, which opened in 1864, are adjacent to each other, divided by the embankment of the East Lancashire Railway. This embankment formed a substantial boundary of Miller Park. In less skilful hands it could have been most unsightly, but in Milner's design it was planted with a variety of trees and shrubs and became one of the most attractive features of the park.

While the cotton famine was of considerable local importance to park development in Lancashire in the 1860s, a more general stimulus came from the work of the Commons Preservation Society (CPS), founded in 1865. As its name implies, the CPS was set up in order to preserve commons and open spaces near large towns. One of its achievements was the saving of Epping Forest in Essex, near London. Initially its attentions were focused on the London commons, but

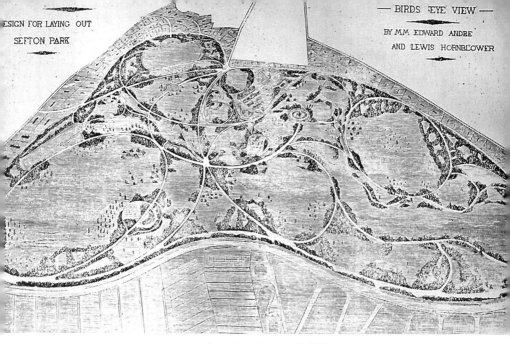

Sefton Park, Liverpool, 1867.

it subsequently broadened its aims to cover the large towns of England and Wales. The CPS was important to park development because it raised public awareness across Britain of the need to preserve open space for recreation.

Alphand, André and the parks of Paris

The dominating influence on park design in Britain in the first decades of the park movement was Joseph Paxton. In France meanwhile J.-C.-A. Alphand had been laying out the parks of Paris as part of Baron Haussmann's sweeping redesign of the city. Among those he laid out were the Bois de Boulogne, Les Buttes-Chaumont and the Parc Monsouris and in them he was assisted by a young landscape architect, Edouard André. André introduced Parisian principles of park design to Britain when in 1867 he won the competition to design Sefton Park, Liverpool, with Lewis Hornblower, who had designed various buildings in Birkenhead Park. The competitors were asked to preserve the longest vistas in the park so as to increase its apparent extent. Vistas could be terminated by the spires of churches outside the park, or by bandstands, refreshment rooms and other structures in the park. The site was undulating, with a valley down the centre, and here André created cascades which led down to the lake. His most important innovation, however, was in the layout of the paths and drives, which took the form of curves and ellipses. These provided the structure of the design, outlining the spaces for various activities, which were screened by planting. The strong similarities in design between Sefton Park and Les Buttes-Chaumont and the Parc Monsouris illustrate Alphand's influence on André.

André's design principles at Sefton Park provided a logical solution to the problem of accommodating a variety of sports and other activities within the elliptical and circular spaces, and fragmentation was prevented by the skill of the whole design. Two parks, Stamford Park in Altrincham and West Park in Wolverhampton, were influenced by this design and in both significant attempts were made to integrate a range of sports facilities within the design of the park. At Stamford Park, designed by John Shaw of Manchester in 1879 and laid out by his son, also John Shaw, elliptical and teardrop spaces are provided for playgrounds, tennis, croquet, cricket and football. Even the bathing pond was elliptical. The competition for the design of West Park, Wolverhampton, was won by Richard Vertegans of Chad Valley Nurseries, Birmingham, in 1879 and the park opened in 1881. His design was based on similar principles of the spaces for the various activities being framed by footpaths and planting, although elliptical forms were not so strictly adhered to.

West Park, Wolverhampton: a flower garden sheltered and visually enclosed by trees.

Another influence occurring in the late 1870s was the reintroduction by William Barron of more formal axial elements into park
design. William Barron was apprenticed at Edinburgh Botanic
Gardens before he became head gardener for Lord Carrington at
Elvaston Castle, Derbyshire. He opened his own nursery and
landscape-gardening business in Borrowash, Derbyshire, in the 1850s
and after his death this was carried on by his son as a successful
company working on both public and private parks and gardens.
Unlike Paxton's use of the terrace, Barron's formality lay in the
plan. At Locke Park, Barnsley (1877), the simple axial plan used a
fountain as the focal point, but in a way that is quite unlike Niven's
geometric plan at Fountains Garden, Paisley, for a winding path
formed the spine of the design. Barron won the competition for
the design of Abbey Park, Leicester, in 1878. There the sophisticated
axial design is hardly evident as one walks around the park, but
the plan clearly shows the axis running through the centre of the
design. The park opened in 1882 and, although Barron did not
indicate the location of particular activities on this plan, the design
included an archery ground, lawn tennis courts, a cricket ground
and a bowling green. This formal approach to design adopted by
Barron was further developed by Thomas Mawson at the turn of
the century.

Locke Park, Barnsley, c.1900: ribbon planting alongside the winding central path.

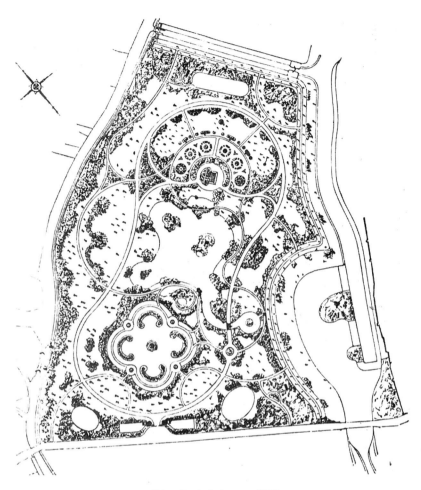

Abbey Park, Leicester, 1880.

Pattern of park development

Park development increased steadily in the middle years of the century, but it was only after 1875 that a substantial increase in activity became evident. The Public Health Act 1875 was the first major Act enabling local authorities to acquire and maintain land for recreation and raise government loans to do so. It marks the point when all the legal difficulties were finally removed, for hitherto each application had required individual legislation, a cumbersome and expensive process. As local authorities acquired the powers to enable them to confront the major urban problems, so their confidence grew and with this increased confidence came an increased sense of civic consciousness and pride. This pride showed

Southport Municipal Gardens, c.1900.

itself in the acquisition of parks and in a variety of features within individual parks.

In the late nineteenth century the park movement broadened when seaside towns, small towns and suburbs started developing parks. In seaside towns and resorts such as Brighton, Blackpool and Scarborough parks were seen as being part of the attractions offered to visitors, rather than as lungs of fresh air in a polluted city, or as places for the social, moral and physical improvement of working people. When the council laid out Marine Park in South Shields in 1890 they were congratulated by the *Gardeners' Chronicle* for their enterprise in adding to the attractions of the town. Indeed, according to other commentators the decorations were so lavish that one might have been mistaken in thinking that a royal visit was imminent.

In London the initial advantage of the royal parks had been followed by the creation of a number of public parks during the early part of the park movement, but the great upsurge in park creation occurred towards the end of the nineteenth century. Until the London County Council was set up in 1888 the main pressure for park creation and the preservation of open space in London came from organisations such as the Commons Preservation Society, the Metropolitan Public Gardens Association, the Corporation of the

City of London and from the actions of benefactors and entrepreneurs. The City of London initiated its open spaces policy in 1878 and among the spaces it acquired and still maintains are Queen's Park, Brent (1887), West Ham Park, Newham (1899) and Epping Forest, for which the CPS had campaigned vigorously. Its income for the preservation of open space came from a tax of three-sixteenths of an old penny on every hundredweight of grain imported into the City of London.

Inner-city parks

During its first decades the park movement tended to concentrate on large prestige projects located mainly on the outskirts of towns. Gradually it was recognised that these parks were inaccessible to the majority of urban dwellers who did not happen to live close to them and that there was a need for small, more accessible inner-city parks and gardens. The movement to create small parks and recreation grounds in inner-city areas dates from the 1880s. Open space in the inner cities had been built over as towns expanded and the population grew, but the churchyards and burial grounds remained and had become increasingly overcrowded. The Burial Act 1853 provided powers for churchyards to be closed, but as no provisions were made for their maintenance they fell into disrepair and decay and the private unconsecrated cemeteries were in an even worse condition. The Open Spaces Act 1881 and the Disused Burial Grounds Act 1884 gave local authorities the powers to transform disused churchyards and burial grounds into gardens and recreation grounds. The conversion of the graveyards of St Paul's Cathedral into open space for recreation dates from this period. The new gardens were designed by Edward Milner and opened in 1879.

A number of organisations like the Manchester and Salford Sanitary Association and the Metropolitan Public Gardens Association (MPGA) in London became involved in the creation of parks and gardens out of disused churchyards, cemeteries and burial grounds. The MPGA had been set up in 1882 by Lord Brabazon, who was particularly concerned with the physical condition of the urban population and the role that parks and playgrounds could play in improving it. Its aim was to acquire disused burial grounds, waste ground and enclosed squares in the most densely populated areas, lay them out as gardens and playgrounds and then hand them over to the local authority. They lost no time in putting their aims into effect. Headstones were moved to the edge of the sites, the ground was levelled and planted and playgrounds were installed in a large number of churchyards. Meath Gardens (1894), created out of the site of the notorious Victoria Park Cemetery, was laid out by the MPGA with a garden, cricket, football and tennis grounds and two large playgrounds, one for boys, the other for girls. The landscape gardeners for the Association were Fanny R. Wilkinson and J. Forsyth Johnson.

Other organisations were also involved. The London Parochial Charities created Postman's Park, one of the largest public parks in the City, out of three disused burial grounds. The park was so called because it was near to London's chief sorting office and was much used by postal workers. Postman's Park was purchased by public subscription in 1900 and commemorated Queen Victoria's Diamond Jubilee. In it is a shelter which was devised and paid for by the painter G. F. Watts and contains about fifty plaques, each with superb lettering, set in the wall. They are a poignant and unique memorial to the actions of ordinary men and women who gave their lives saving others.

Although these churchyards and burial grounds had been very neglected there was a difference between how they were treated and what people felt about them. Most people at that time regarded such places with awe and reverence. The idea that they should be transformed into playgrounds, with children 'romping about in churchyards and turning somersaults on the graves, was (to some)

Postman's Park, London: the commemorative plaques.

too revolting and disagreeable to contemplate'. Their transformation into gardens and recreation grounds represented a very radical change in thinking, particularly in view of the religious feelings of the period. Although they did not add large areas of open space for recreation, their amenity value was of enormous significance to those living nearby, particularly the aged and the very young.

Open spaces movement

While these small inner-city parks were being created, attention was being drawn to the need to acquire land for parks on the outskirts of towns. Transport was improving, working hours were being reduced and the newly introduced bank holidays provided more opportunities for longer journeys. If these sites were chosen because of their natural beauty they tended to be left in their natural state as far as possible. When William Goldring designed Endcliffe Wood outside Sheffield for public use, he was asked to preserve its natural state as far as possible.

With the growing opportunities for travel and continued urban expansion came moves to preserve the countryside. The CPS had worked for many years to protect the countryside and commons near towns, but they could not buy land to preserve it as open space. Octavia Hill suggested that a trust should be formed to protect historic sites and the countryside and in 1895 the National Trust

St Luke's recreation ground, Chelsea, London.

for Historic Sites and Natural Scenery was set up. It had a direct link with the CPS for the Trust's first chairman was Sir Robert Hunter of the CPS.

The Golden and Diamond Jubilees of Queen Victoria in 1887 and 1897 further stimulated park development. In many towns these events were marked by gifts or by subscriptions raised from the community, which contributed towards the acquisition of new parks. Other important national events such as the coronations of Edward VII in 1902 and of George V in 1911 provided additional impetus. The cost of open space in or near built-up areas was inevitably high and forward planning was necesssary if open space for recreation was to be made available before an area was developed. The Town Planning Act of 1909 provided a formal mechanism for this, but parks still tended to be acquired in an *ad hoc* rather than a planned way and local authorities continued to be the main providers of parks.

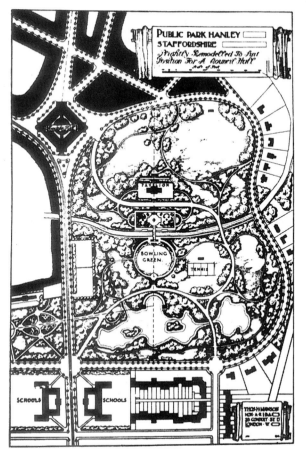

Plan of Hanley Park, Stoke-on-Trent, 1891.

Parks in the twentieth century

Mawson and his influence

The years 1830-85 were the pioneering period of park creation. By 1885 park development was assured and many more parks were created in the period 1885-1914 than in the pioneering phase. In the period before the First World War the concern with fresh air, physical health and mortality rates was reinforced by concern for the health of young people and the need for facilities for active recreation. The Inter-Departmental Committee Report on Physical Deterioration, published in 1904, marked official recognition of the problem and further evidence came from medical reports on prospective army recruits for the Boer War and for the First World War. The resulting pressure led to the setting up of such organisations as the National Playing Fields Association. By 1910 the Metropolitan Public Gardens Association was adopting the principle that playing fields were of primary importance. In the inter-war period a large number of playing fields were created, many of them commemorating George V and called 'King George V Playing Fields'. The momentum of park development was maintained between the two world wars; indeed Glasgow acquired half of its parks after 1925 and the pattern of park development there was not radically different from that in other large cities.

Joseph Paxton had been the most influential figure in the early years of the park movement and Thomas Mawson became the leading figure in park design in the period 1890-1933, not only for the number of parks that he designed, but also because his ideas received wide circulation through his writings and lectures. After working with a well-known nursery and landscape-gardening company in London, Mawson set up a company in the Lake District, where he specialised in both private and public parks and gardens. He became President of the Town Planning Institute in 1923, was a founder member of the Royal Fine Art Commission in the same year and was elected first President of the Institute of Landscape Architects in 1929. The main principle of Mawson's designs was a formal core which was then set in landscaped surroundings. His first public park commission was for the design of Hanley Park, Stoke-on-Trent, in 1891, and the park opened in 1898. The site was a difficult one, with clay pits, disused mineshafts, spoil banks and a canal flowing through it from east to west. The plan (opposite page) shows how Mawson made a strong central axis running south from

*Belle Vue
Park,
Newport,
Gwent.*

the pavilion, which is set on a terrace, across the lake to a small pavilion on the opposite bank of the lake. A second axis can be seen in the south-west corner, running across the Cauldon Gardens to the boathouse. These axes provided the formal core and the curving walks which defined the different areas were set within this frame. Around the edge of the park the raised ground planted with fast-growing trees screened the industrial surroundings from view. The lake was supplied by water which ran through a dell, with rockwork cascades constructed by James Pulham. Pulham was celebrated for his skill in creating artificial rockwork that was so convincing that it fooled even geologists.

In many of Mawson's designs the formal core of the park is set in landscaped surroundings of great imagination and sensitivity. Belle Vue Park, Newport, Gwent (1892), is set on a steeply sloping site which commands excellent views over the estuary. The terracotta

Waterloo Park, Norwich: pergola and herbaceous border.

pavilion and terrace garden at the top of the site provided the formal emphasis to the design, while lower down the intimate planting around the cascade contrasted with the open areas of grass and the surrounding trees. Mawson was involved in the design of many parks, but not all his proposals were carried out. For example, in 1903 he put forward plans with Patrick Geddes for laying out Pittencrieff Park in Dunfermline; some, but not all, of their ideas were put into effect when the park was laid out by James Whitton of the Glasgow Botanic Gardens. Mawson's influence was continued by others such as Captain A. Sandys Winch, who designed five parks in Norwich in the 1920s and 1930s. One of the five, Waterloo Park, which opened in 1933, featured a 100 metres long herbaceous border leading to a pavilion, a yew-hedged bowling green and a central garden with a bandstand set in a moat of pools and rills. These were subsequently filled in and used as flower beds. The north and south sides of the central garden are bounded by pergolas which were covered with climbing roses and other plants.

Other well-known garden designers and landscape architects who also worked on public parks in the twentieth century include Percy Cane and Sir Geoffrey Jellicoe. King George's Park (formerly Southfields Park), Wandsworth, was laid out by Percy Cane and opened in 1923. It was further developed both before and after the Second World War and featured an ornamental garden with winding footpaths, lime avenue, rockery and heather garden. Sir Geoffrey Jellicoe was President of the Institute of Landscape Architects from 1939 to 1949 and became founder President of the International Federation of Landscape Architects in 1948. He was knighted for his services to the profession. His international practice ranged from town planning to private gardens and in Britain his largest projects included town plans for Hemel Hempstead (one of London's new towns), Guildford and Gloucester. The water gardens at Hemel Hempstead illustrate Jellicoe's imaginative use of water as a design element.

Despite the tendency to focus on the better-known designers of public parks, their contribution in terms of the total number of parks created across Britain was very small. By far the majority of public parks were designed by borough engineers and surveyors, nurserymen and park superintendents. Three park superintendents stand out: J. W. McHattie, who was in charge of the Edinburgh parks and has been credited with the introduction of the floral clock; W. W. Pettigrew, who laid out Roath Park (1894) in Cardiff, became superintendent of the Manchester parks from 1915 to 1932 and wrote the first textbook on public park management, *Municipal Parks: Layout, Management and Administration* (London, 1937); and Lieutenant-Colonel J. J. Sexby, the first chief officer of the London County Council Parks Department and author of *The Municipal Parks, Gardens and Open Spaces of London*, 1895. Sexby was in charge of all the municipal parks, gardens and open spaces in London maintained by the LCC and had a staff of one thousand. Of these 503 were trained gardeners and 320 were park-keepers who patrolled the parks and kept order.

Outstanding amongst the many borough engineers and surveyors involved in park design and layout was William Louis de Normanville, who was borough surveyor and engineer of Leamington Spa between 1882 and 1917. One of the greatest attractions of Leamington is the river Leam, which runs through the centre of the town, with a chain of parks, gardens and walks alongside it. De Normanville undertook engineering works to control the river, built three bridges across it, laid out Victoria Park, which opened in 1898, and created the York Promenade and Mill Gardens on the south side of the river, opposite the Pump Room Gardens and Jephson Gardens, which were already in existence. He also built the Pump Room Swimming Baths, renovated the Pump Rooms and modernised the sewers. The Victorian landscape that de Normanville created still survives today at the heart of Leamington.

Local architects worked on the design of parks, but few nationally known architects were involved. This is surprising considering the impact in the Edwardian period of architects such as Edwin Lutyens on the design of private gardens. C. F. A. Voysey seems to have been the only well-known architect to have been involved in public park design. He designed the Emslie Horniman Pleasance in North Kensington, London, which opened in 1914.

While women were making a name for themselves in the design of private gardens, few designed public parks. An exception was Fanny Wilkinson, who was involved with the Metropolitan Public Gardens Association. She was the designer of Vauxhall Park, Lambeth (1890). Myatt's Fields, Lambeth (1889), which was acquired by the MPGA, was probably also laid out by her.

After the Second World War

After the end of the Second World War the emphasis of town planning in Britain was on slum clearance, urban renewal, zoning and applying Le Corbusier's ideas for the city of the future. In practice this too often meant systems-built high-rise housing, but Le Corbusier's ideas for setting these high-rise blocks in luxuriant parkland with wonderful sporting facilities were seldom put into effect. New parks were not a priority in this planning process. After 1945 the influence of modernism, suspended during the war, extended not only to architecture and town planning, but also to parks, and existing parks began to suffer from its influence. One aspect of modernism was a preference for undecorated features. Translated to parks, this meant replacing massed displays of flowers and ornate planting with bold sweeps of grass, the equivalent of clean-sweep planning. The resulting 'green deserts', as they have been so aptly called, had the advantage of being more cheaply and easily maintained, but they were very much less interesting for the park visitor to look at.

One area of new park development in the post-war period was in the new towns, which were created during the 1950s and 1960s. In the early years of the twentieth century the influence of model industrial villages such as Port Sunlight and Bournville and the

Pump Room Gardens, Leamington Spa, c.1900.

building of the first garden city at Letchworth had encouraged the development of garden cities and garden suburbs. One of the main principles of the garden city movement was that adequate provision of parks and other forms of open space should be included in the plan from the outset and this influence continued through to the new towns which developed in the 1950s and 1960s.

The decline of urban parks

During the Second World War the gates and railings of many parks were removed as a contribution to the war effort. While this may have made a psychological contribution, it did not apparently make a practical one, for they are reputed to have been dumped in the Atlantic Ocean. Other gates and railings have been stolen or deliberately removed more recently and it is impossible to protect parks against theft and vandalism unless they can be locked at night. The effect of this loss of gates and railings was not immediate, but it began to be felt when the actions taken by central government in the 1970s took effect. The reorganisation of local government and the merging of Parks Departments with Leisure Services, which was recommended in the Bains Report of 1972, posed far greater threats to public parks. As a result of this reorganisation Parks Departments not only lost their identity, but they had to compete with Leisure Services for their budget and a budget for parks was not included in the government's Standard Spending Assessment formula. This formula determines the Revenue Support Grant for each local authority and this takes no account of the actual costs of park management for which each local authority is responsible. The maintenance of public parks has always been a service, for the parks generate little revenue for their owners, the local authorities. Because park maintenance is not a statutory responsibility, local authority budget cuts, in response to pressure from central government and the threat of rate capping if they overspend, have often fallen on parks.

Another factor which contributed to the decline of urban parks came as a result of the countryside legislation of 1970, which included the creation of the Countryside Commission. For the first time grants became available to set up country parks, with countryside rangers, and large numbers of new country parks were opened on the outskirts of towns and in open country. Because grants were available for country parks the attention of local authorities became focused on them, to the detriment of urban parks. Moreover, their maintenance costs were low and they were popular with the car-owning public.

People's Park, Halifax, 1993. Statues are encased in hardboard to prevent further vandalism.

The creation of country parks on the edge of towns is part of the same process of decentralising and weakening town centres which the creation of out-of-town shopping malls has encouraged.

A further factor promoting the decline of urban parks resulted from the Local Government Act 1988. The established methods of park maintenance with park-keepers attached to each park were replaced by a requirement that all services be put out to tender. Compulsory Competitive Tendering meant that, instead of Parks Departments continuing to be responsible for park maintenance, they became the clients who specified and monitored what should be done. As a result park-keepers, who had been a constant presence in the parks, disappeared and in their place came contractors who were responsible for a number of parks and were thus a much less evident presence in all of them. Nursery work, apprenticeship and training in horticulture were all associated with and part of the traditional management of urban parks and these have also disappeared as a result of this new regime. The long-term effect of the lack of training in this area has yet to be felt. The individual character of each park comes from its location, its design and landscaping, the planting, buildings, statues and memorials. By the mid 1990s the impact of these detrimental factors on the fabric of parks had become increasingly evident.

The main entrance of Birkenhead Park, 1847.

Shelters, palm houses and other buildings

Lodges

The first building the park visitor encountered was often the lodge by the entrance gate, with the park regulations displayed prominently nearby. The lodges housed the park-keepers and superintendents who looked after the park and opened and closed the gates each morning and evening. These buildings set the tone for the park within and proclaimed that it was a special place, separate and different from its urban surroundings. Many parks had several entrances, each with a lodge. In Birkenhead Park each lodge was in a different architectural style, adding variety to the park. The Gothic Lodge was, despite its name, Tudor in style; there was also an Italian Lodge with a belvedere, a Castellated Lodge, and a pair of Norman Lodges, which were small Greek Revival buildings flanking one of the entrances. The grandest of the buildings, however, was the main entrance, which consisted of a triumphal arch, flanked by two small archways linked to lodges on either side. The central arch was for carriages and the two side ones for pedestrians.

Park lodges were a feature of both nineteenth- and twentieth-century parks and their design, like that of the other buildings in parks, tended either to reflect current tastes in architecture or to refer to local architectural styles. Lodges in the Picturesque, the Gothic Revival, the Classical, the High Victorian Gothic and the English Vernacular Revival styles could be found gracing the entrances of parks throughout Britain. At Baxter Park, Dundee, the lodge was in the Scottish Baronial style, while at Mesnes Park, Wigan (1878), a Swiss style was favoured. At Grosvenor Park, Chester (1867), the half-timbered lodge by John Douglas included carvings of the Norman Earls of Chester and related to the characteristic black and white architecture of the town.

These lodges stood beside entrance gates that were often very elaborate and both reinforced the significance of the park. Manufacturers of cast iron, such as Walter Macfarlane of Glasgow, provided a complete range of park furnishings, including entrance gates and the railings that fenced the park, seats, shelters, ornamental fountains, bandstands, clock-towers, urinals and kick-rails to keep people from walking on the grass. Mass-production meant that costs could be kept low, provided sufficient quantities were manufactured. These products found their way not only into the parks of Britain but also into the parks that

Baxter Park, Dundee: this lodge at the south entrance has been pulled down.

Queen's Park, Crewe, 1888: the entrance lodge and gates. The park was the gift of the London & North Western Railway Company.

Prince's Park, Liverpool, 1844: the entrance gates. This was Paxton's first public park, but by the mid 1990s it was in a very bad condition.

were created widely across the British Empire.

Towards the end of the 1980s park lodges began to be seen by local authorities both as a maintenance problem and as a potential asset to be realised. As a result of Compulsory Competitive Tendering there were no longer any park-keepers to live in the lodges, for resident park-keepers had been replaced by peripatetic workers who came intermittently to cut the grass and maintain the park. The lack of resident park-keepers meant that there was no one in the parks to police them and people, especially women and children, became increasingly fearful of using some parks. In many instances the lodges have been pulled down, boarded up, rented or sold to people who had nothing to do with the park, for hard-pressed councils were constantly looking for ways to save money. The message on entering the park is consequently very different.

Shelters and refreshment rooms

Shelters, refreshment rooms, toilets and drinking fountains enabled people to spend long hours in the park, which would not otherwise have been possible. The types of building to be found in parks and the ways in which they were used related to the whole question of recreation and the activities that were permitted in parks. Generally park buildings such as the lodges, shelters and boathouses were small in scale so that they did not intrude on or dominate their surroundings and many of them are delightful structures. Large buildings did feature in parks, particularly in those that were created out of the gardens of an existing mansion. It was then necessary to find a role for them that was compatible with the uses of the park. A common solution was to provide refreshment rooms in them, but alcohol was usually prohibited in such places and they were often closed during the time of church services on Sunday, in order to encourage people to go to church. Another solution was to use them for educational activities such as a museum, library or art gallery and this conformed with the educational aspirations of the park promoters. Manchester's record in this area has been sustained into the 1990s and the City Art Gallery has branches located in five public parks.

Park buildings drew not only on national architectural styles but also on those of other cultures, reflecting a picturesque interest in variety as well as Britain's imperial role. Garden buildings in the Chinese taste had become fashionable in England in the mid eighteenth century and the Ranelagh and Vauxhall pleasure gardens both featured Chinese pavilions. Sir William Chambers was a keen advocate of landscape gardening in the Chinese taste and his pagoda (1761-2) still survives in Kew Gardens. Interest in the pagoda and in Chinese buildings continued into the nineteenth century and the Chinese pavilion in Riverside Gardens, Belper, Derbyshire, is still a feature. Both Victoria Park, London, and Birkenhead Park

Sefton Park, Liverpool: lakeside shelter.

had examples set on islands in the lakes. In Birkenhead Park the pagoda served as a shelter and was reached by means of a Chinese bridge. Neither of them exists today. In Birkenhead there is also a Swiss bridge, while in Peel Park, Salford, the Victoria Arch, built in 1859 to commemorate Queen Victoria's second visit to the park, featured Indian elements in its horseshoe arches and ogee-shaped finials. This interest continues today, for example in the Chinese Friendship Garden with its little bridges, Chinese-patterned red and gold railings and small pagoda, which opened in Abbey Park, Leicester, in 1989.

Parks also featured ruins and fragments of buildings, some of which were inherited and others acquired as a result of demolition, road improvements or new building developments. In 1931 Abbey Park, Leicester, was extended by the donation of the site of the ruins of the abbey where Cardinal Wolsey had died in 1530, together with a piece of ground known as the Oval. The boundary wall of the Oval contains a section known as Abbot Penny's Wall, reputed to be the oldest brick wall in England and built in 1345-77. Mobray Park, Sunderland, contains a Norman archway from the Bishopwearmouth Rectory which was demolished in 1856, while in that part of Grosvenor Park, Chester, that was formerly a quarry are the remains of a Gothic abbey. Marsden Park in Nelson, Lancashire, was formed out of the grounds of the mid eighteenth-century Marsden Hall. In the early nineteenth century the owner built a number of extraordinary structures in the grounds including an ornamental arch of mixed Gothic and Classical forms. Amongst the most unusual of these structures is a polygonal sundial made

Christchurch Park, Ipswich, 1895: shelter.

Abbey Park, Leicester: refreshment pavilion, c.1890. This photograph was taken soon after the park was opened; the trees are still quite young.

Abbey Park, Leicester: Chinese Friendship Garden, 1989.

Sefton Park, Liverpool: the palm house with the figure of Mercator, the 'Father of Modern Cartography'.

Glasgow Botanic Gardens: inside the Kibble Conservatory, c.1900.

by Thornber & Kipps (1841), with twenty faces, each with a gnomon. Each face was supposed to tell the time in different parts of the world, provided the sun was shining.

Palm houses

Towards the end of the nineteenth century palm houses were added to a number of parks. The use of palm houses and conservatories to provide a climate in which to grow exotic and tender plants had been well-known for half a century, but they were expensive to build. The palm houses designed by Mackenzie and Moncur in Sefton Park and Stanley Park, Liverpool, were both donated by the millionaire Henry Yates Thompson and opened in 1896 and 1899 respectively. In Glasgow John Kibble's large private conservatory was moved to the Botanic Gardens in 1871 and Kibble was given a free lease to use it for 'elevating entertainment'. As this venture proved unsuccessful the corporation took over the building twenty years later for use as a winter garden. Palm houses extended the use of the park in cold and wet weather in a way that was quite different from that offered by the traditional shelters. Visitors were introduced to new tropical and subtropical plants in 'a fairy-land of graceful palms, orange, cotton and banana trees', and the experience of light and foliage inside was quite different from that outside.

Many palm houses suffered from damage or destruction during the Second World War and after the war those that survived began increasingly to deteriorate. By the end of the 1980s the high costs of maintenance and vandalism caused many to be closed. To solve the problems of costs, alternative uses were sought: for example, the Gladstone Conservatory in Stanley Park, Liverpool, reopened in 1989 as a licensed bar, restaurant and social centre after complete refurbishment, including double glazing. However, it did not survive long in this new role. Sefton Park's palm house was by the early 1990s in a very poor state, lacking its glass and the statues that stood around it. It became the subject of an imaginative fund-raising proposal led by George Melly whereby people were invited to contribute to individual panes of glass, but by the mid 1990s its future was still uncertain.

Most of these building types could be found in private parks, where they developed initially. The one type of park building that had no counterpart in private parks was the bandstand, and it, above all, has come to be associated with the public park.

Entertainment and education

The bandstand

By the end of the nineteenth century bandstands had become so popular that no park was considered complete without one. The first bandstands, or band houses as they were then called, were built in the Royal Horticultural Society Gardens, Kensington, which opened in 1861. One of them was moved in 1890 to Clapham Common, London, where it still stands. These bandstands were designed by Captain Francis Fowke of the Royal Engineers, the designer of the main quadrangle of the Victoria and Albert Museum and of the Royal Albert Hall. They were circular domed pavilions supported by slender cast-iron columns. Fowke may well have seen a similar pavilion when he was working in Paris for one was displayed at the Paris Industrial Exhibition, which opened in May 1855. The form is similar to that of the *chatri*, the domed and pillared pavilion that is a feature of many Indian and Islamic buildings.

Music had been played in parks before bandstands were introduced, but bandstands provided a focus and they quickly became very popular. People either sat on seats or deckchairs to listen or strolled around, but, unlike bandstands in pleasure gardens, those

Clapham Common, London: the bandstand.

Queen's Park, Brent, London: the restored bandstand.

in public parks were rarely the focus for dancing until the twentieth century. Concerts by military and works bands were held on weekday evenings and Sundays in the summer and they were enormously popular, but the playing of music on Sundays was subject to opposition from such groups as the Sabbatarians and the Lord's Day Observance Society. When eleven brass bands gathered on the upper terrace of Corporation Park, Blackburn, in 1861, more than fifty thousand people gathered to listen. A wide range of classical music was performed and music was considered to be an important positive influence. The bandstand was seen as another aspect of the reforming potential of parks.

Manufacturers provided a wide range of designs and some, such as Walter Macfarlane of Glasgow, provided catalogues illustrating the various types and stating where particular designs had been erected. Bandstands were available not only in cast iron: rustic bandstands of wood also became very popular. They continued to be built in parks between the wars when concrete, the 'new' fashionable material, was used. After the Second World War, however, tastes changed. Not only were no more bandstands built, but as the fabric of the surviving ones deteriorated they tended to be removed. Those that did survive and were well maintained during the 1970s and

The bandstand in Alexandra Park, Hastings.

The refurbished bandstand in Abbey Grounds, Hexham, Northumberland.

early 1980s began to suffer at the end of that decade and by the mid 1990s many bandstands had become derelict and boarded up.

Many of these buildings have been vandalised, have disappeared or are in poor condition and some local authorities would like to accelerate this process of attrition. According to a report presented by one council in 1995, 'Park buildings are a maintenance liability and can attract vandalism. They can also be visually intrusive and will be reduced to the minimum needed, consistent with the effective management of the parks. Where listed buildings exist they will, if possible, be found a long term use. Other buildings will be progressively eliminated.' According to another local authority, the charming Edwardian wooden shelter in one of its parks was 'socially and functionally obsolete' because it attracted vandals!

In addition to having their existing buildings vandalised, parks have in the 1980s and 1990s become the target of a number of building developments. These range from the large new leisure centre built in one corner of Tollcross Park, Glasgow, to sheltered housing built on part of Bitton Park, Teignmouth, Devon, and the building of a large garden centre in Rouken Glen Park, Glasgow. Road developments have also taken large slices of a number of parks.

Drinking fountains
If people were to spend lengthy periods in a park drinking water was essential, particularly for children. Indeed, before the provision of free drinking fountains they could be found crowding round the

Sefton Park, Liverpool: bas-relief on the Samuel Smith obelisk and drinking fountain.

cab stands and drinking out of the pails of water with the horses. In London the Metropolitan Free Drinking Fountain Association was set up in 1859 by the Quaker Samuel Gurney. It later started supplying cattle and horse troughs and changed its name in 1867 to the Metropolitan Drinking Fountain and Cattle Trough Association. The Association was closely connected with the temperance movement and many granite fountains inscribed and donated by the Association can still be found in London's parks. Drinking fountains provided an ideal opportunity for promoting temperance and the delights of drinking water. In the People's Park, Halifax, the drinking fountain is inscribed on one side 'Thank God for water' and on the other 'Water is best'. In Sefton Park, Liverpool, the obelisk commemorating Samuel Smith MP, philanthropist and friend of India, has a drinking fountain at its base and some fine bas-reliefs which bore the inscription 'He who drinks here shall still thirst, but he who drinks of God shall thirst no more'. These reliefs have been stolen. One of the most imposing drinking fountains is the Victoria Fountain in Victoria Park, London, donated by Baroness Angela Burdett-Coutts, designed by Henry Darbishire and installed in 1862. It has red granite piers, a cupola covered in red and purple slates, with four cherubs seated on dolphins under it, and the inscriptions 'Temperance is a bridle of gold' and 'The earth is the Lord's and all that therein is'. It was restored in the early 1990s.

Parks provided many opportunities for promoting education and cultivating virtue and their effectiveness was 'proved' statistically in Macclesfield. An article published in the *Transactions of the National Association for the Promotion of Social Science* in 1857 noted that three years after the opening of West Park in 1854 drunkenness and disorderly conduct had decreased by 23 per cent, gambling by 50 per cent and the use of profane language by 60 per cent!

Prehistory

In the years before and after Charles Darwin published *The Origin of Species* in 1859 the interest in studying all aspects of the natural world, past and present, was widespread. Collecting and classification were important first steps before any scientific theory could be presented and this interest in the natural world was not confined to the plants and animals in existence at the time but included the distant world of prehistory. A number of parks displayed fossilised remains, some of which had been discovered when the park was being created. In Victoria Park, Glasgow (1887), a grove of ten fossilised trunks and roots of trees was revealed when the park

Victoria Fountain, Victoria Park, London.

Crystal Palace Park: the megalosaurus, a large carnivore.

was being laid out by unemployed shipbuilding workers and they became part of the attractions of the park. Fossilised tree trunks were displayed in Horton Park, Bradford, and in Sheffield Botanic Gardens, but today they are often unlabelled and can easily be missed.

The largest and most dramatic of all these prehistoric displays is to be found in Crystal Palace Park. The fossilised remains of animals that had been discovered by the mid nineteenth century consisted mainly of fragments and few people had any idea of how these animals might have looked or how large they were. At Crystal Palace Park life-sized reconstructions of fourteen different prehistoric species from 600 million years of prehistory were displayed for the first time anywhere. They included models of the labyrinthodon, one of the earliest land animals, the teleosaurus, the megalosaurus, the iguanodon, pterodactyls and mammals such as the megaceros. These were displayed among models of plants which would have existed at the time, on geological islands which showed strata, for geology was another very popular interest. These prehistoric animals were built under the guidance of Professor Richard Owen, who established prehistory as an academic discipline and who introduced the word 'dinosaur' to the language. They were depicted according to the

The banquet in the iguanodon on New Year's Eve, 1853.

latest research and constructed by the artist and sculptor Benjamin Waterhouse Hawkins from shells of brick, reinforced with iron and faced with stucco. To celebrate their completion Waterhouse Hawkins organised a grand banquet in the mould of the iguanodon under a tent at the Crystal Palace Park on New Year's Eve 1853. The guest of honour, Professor Owen, was seated at the head of the table in the head of the iguanodon and the twenty guests in the body. Subsequent research has modified our knowledge of the form of these animals, but there is no intention of altering or updating them for they represent a milestone in popularising the history of science and they can still be enjoyed in their original environment on islands in the park. Near the islands strata of coal, millstone grit, sandstone, ironstone and limestone are displayed and further along was a working replica of a Derbyshire lead mine.

Civic and national pride

Parks were places for marking important events. Statues, memorials, commemorative planting and buildings, drinking fountains and sundials provided opportunities for celebrating the achievements or generosity of individuals, the civic pride of the local authority and the national pride of the citizens. They gave each park its special identity and strengthened the links beween the park and its local community. Until the death of Prince Albert in 1861 Queen Victoria travelled extensively on the expanding railway network, visiting towns and opening new buildings and parks. Such visits were often commemorated by erecting a statue of the Queen in the public park. After the death of the Prince, the Queen went into deep mourning and it was not until the 1870s that she began to resume public life. Renewed interest in commissioning statues of the Queen came with her Golden Jubilee in 1887 and Diamond Jubilee in 1897 and many parks acquired statues of her in the following years. Some of these were private gifts; others were paid for by the local authority, but the majority were funded by public subscription and so involved the local community, or parts of it.

One of the grandest fountains celebrating Victoria as Queen and Empress is the Doulton Fountain. It was the largest terracotta statue in the world at the time it was installed in Kelvingrove Park, Glasgow, for the International Exhibition of 1888. In 1890 it was moved to Glasgow Green, where it still stands. The subject of the fountain is Queen Victoria reigning over her Empire. At the top is the Queen wearing the Imperial Crown and holding an orb and sceptre. Below are two basins, the lower one with four groups representing India, South Africa, Canada and Australia and the main resources of those countries. At the centre of the upper basin are four figures – a sailor and Scottish, Irish and English soldiers – representing the power of the British army and navy that made the Empire possible. By the mid 1990s the fountain was in a very poor condition.

The figures of the Queen and Prince Albert were accompanied by statues, obelisks, fountains and other buildings commemorating local members of Parliament, aristocrats, entrepreneurs and park donors. Locke Park in Barnsley (1862) is one of the few parks donated by a woman – Phoebe Locke. Her gift and the gift by her sister of an adjoining piece of land were commemorated by a tower erected in Locke Park in 1877. One of the most imposing commemorative park buildings must be the Edwardian baroque

The Doulton Fountain, Glasgow Green.

People's Park, Halifax, 1910. The original (Paxton) fountain with the terrace and pavilion behind.

Ashton Memorial in Williamson Park, Lancaster (1896). It was designed by John Belcher and J. J. Joass in 1906-9 and has been called 'the grandest monument in England'. The donor of the park, James Williamson, had made his fortune from the manufacture of linoleum and his son, who later became Lord Ashton, commissioned the building as a memorial to his family. It stands in a commanding part of the park and can be seen from miles around. In People's Park, Halifax, a statue of the donor, Sir Francis Crossley, is seated in the Italian loggia. In front of it is the terrace with a series of Classical statues, urns and a Neapolitan dancing girl which framed the view of the park beyond. By the early 1990s People's Park had been so severely vandalised that the local authority enclosed the statues in hardboard (see page 39) until they could decide what action to take and had the necessary funds. Subsequently even the hardboard was vandalised. The park became the subject of a major restoration programme in the mid 1990s.

As well as commemorating individuals, parks reflected local features, local industry and civic pride. Local pride could also be seen in the miniature stone circles or gorsedd rings which stand in Cathays Park, Cardiff, and Victoria Park, Neath, and in such features as the miniature waterfall created in Lister Park, Bradford, *c*.1903, a recreation of the well-known Thornton Force nearby. Liverpool's maritime pride was celebrated in Sefton Park by the figures of James Cook, 'Explorer of Australia', Mercator, 'Father of Modern Cartography', and Henry the Navigator, 'Father of Atlantic Exploration', which were positioned around the palm house. They were accompanied by figures of major importance to gardens and the development of botany: Charles Darwin, John Parkinson, 'Apothecary to James I', and André Le Nôtre, 'the most famous of garden architects'. Inscriptions explained the significance of each figure, so local pride was combined with education. These statues were removed for safe-keeping in the early 1990s. Another example of pride in local achievements is the monument in South Park, Darlington, to John Fowler, who in the mid nineteenth century developed the steam plough.

Civic pride showed itself in the acquisition of parks, as well as in the various features in them. One of the most dramatic expressions of that pride can be seen in the Stewart Memorial Fountain erected in Kelvingrove Park in 1872 to celebrate the bringing of clean water from Loch Katrine to the people of Glasgow. Robert Stewart, the Lord Provost of Glasgow, had fought for many years for the project and it was decided some years after its completion to commemorate his efforts. The competition for the design of the

The Ashton Memorial, Williamson Park, Lancaster.

Stewart Memorial Fountain, Kelvingrove Park, Glasgow, 1872.

memorial was won by James Sellars, who based his design on Sir Walter Scott's poem 'The Lady of the Lake'. The gilded bronze lady crowns the fountain. This was restored in 1988 at a cost of £158,000 but was subsequently revandalised.

Parks and war

Parks reflected both national and international events, and statues and memorials commemorated wars, battles and campaigns. The war that was most widely commemorated in the nineteenth century was the Crimean War and guns from that war were one of the most common features to appear in parks during the late 1850s and early 1860s. Many parks acquired two guns and displayed them with pride. In People's Park, Sunderland, they flanked the statue of Sir Henry Havelock, the son of a Sunderland shipbuilder, who had been sent to Lucknow and Cawnpore in the Indian Mutiny of 1857. In Nottingham Arboretum (1852) two guns from Sebastopol and two replicas and piles of cannonballs were placed around a pagoda. From this pagoda hung a bell taken by the Nottinghamshire Regiment of Foot from a temple in Canton during the Opium Wars. The bell was subsequently given to the East Lancashire Regiment and the cannonballs were removed, as children enjoyed rolling them down the slopes, but park-keepers did not enjoy retrieving them.

Other wars and campaigns were commemorated, but much less widely. A 16 ton lion in Forbury Gardens, Reading, erected in 1886, commemorates the members of the Royal Berkshire Regiment

Nottingham Arboretum: the pagoda and Crimean cannons, c.1900.

Khyber Pass, East Park, Hull, c.1900.

who fell at Maiwand, Kandahar and elsewhere in the Afghan Campaign (1879-80). The role of the Imperial Camel Corps in campaigns in Egypt, Sinai and Palestine in 1916-18 is commemorated in Victoria Embankment Gardens, London, by a statue of a camel with its rider. One of the most unusual forms of commemoration is the miniature Khyber Pass which was constructed by E. A. Peak out of artificial stone as part of the original layout of East Park, Hull (1887). This now lacks its bridge and is in a very dilapidated condition. These structures celebrated victory and the power of the Empire and commemorated the names of regiments and particular battles. It was not until the First and Second World Wars that memorials recorded the names of individuals who lost their lives. Parks were also used for military events such as drilling volunteers. In the 1860s fear of invasion by Napoleon III led to the formation of volunteers in a number of towns and drill took place in parks throughout Britain. It offered a spectacle to visitors and was accepted as being in the national interest.

During the First World War and for a short time afterwards parks displayed both captured enemy tanks and guns and British ones from the War Office, in order to encourage the war effort. Later, when public opinion changed, these were removed but the Crimean guns survived until the Second World War, when many were melted down for munitions. During the Second World War many parks were used as sites for mounting searchlights and barrage balloons. They were also used for food production in both world wars. In Victoria Park, Cardiff, a rabbitry was established in the First World War and during the Second World War the park was used for growing food as part of the Dig for Victory campaign, as were many parks throughout Britain. Parks also contributed to the war effort during the Second World War as part of the Holidays at Home Campaign. In order to conserve resources, travelling was discouraged and a large number of events were put on in parks in the summer holidays to enable families to participate in and enjoy a variety of activities, in *lieu* of taking a holiday.

Parks were used to stage mock battles, which became a popular attraction. One of the earliest examples of these is associated with the Crimean War (1854-6). The press carried detailed reports of the war and nearly every issue of the *Illustrated London News* contained accounts of the conflict. Commercial organisations were quick to take advantage of this interest and in 1855 visitors to the Surrey Zoological Gardens could have a 'Sebastopol Experience'. A large scale model of Sebastopol was built in the pleasure garden, with the forts, the Redan and other features familiar from reports of the siege, and with the fleet blockading the harbour. Troops invalided out of the Crimea mimed sorties, attacks and manoeuvres against a background of fireworks, fizzers and crackers and what seemed like the thunder of artillery.

Mock naval battles, or naumachias, fought between manned model gunships were a feature of private parks during the eighteenth and nineteenth centuries. They were introduced to Peasholm Park, Scarborough, in 1927 by the Entertainments Manager of the local authority, George Horrocks, and in its early days the naumachia recreated First World War engagements. After the Second World War it staged the battle of the River Plate and encounters of the battle of the Atlantic, to a background of fireworks. The naumachias are still staged every summer. The largest of the vessels is over 6 metres (20 feet) long and the spectacle is popular with tourists.

Planting and maintenance

For many park visitors the flowers were the main attraction, but it was not until the 1850s and 1860s that floral displays became an important feature in public parks. In the parks of the 1840s such as Birkenhead Park or those of Manchester and Salford flowers were not a significant feature. The increasing emphasis in parks on flowers, bedding plants and carpet-bedding displays was due partly to the influence of the Crystal Palace Park at Sydenham (1856), designed by Joseph Paxton, partly to the dramatically expanding range of flowering hybrids that became available, and partly the result of the polluted air in the major industrial centres. At Crystal Palace Park the dramatic fountains and waterworks were accompanied by massed bedding plants in the flower beds alongside the walks. Tom Thumb scarlet pelargoniums were planted around the edges of the beds, with paler-coloured plants at the centre so that the beds appeared larger. Salvias, ageratums, heliotropes, petunias and verbenas were seen in profusion. This lavish and dramatic planting was widely reported in the press and it prompted displays of bedding plants in the royal parks and subsequently in the municipal parks. To enable these displays to be seen to advantage, the earth was mounded up in the centre, or the beds were inclined. Another solution was ribbon beds planted on either side of a footpath. The ribbon beds in Locke Park, Barnsley, were planted with ribbons of plants graded in height, one species for each strand of the ribbon. This ribbon bedding in Locke Park was continued until 1991, when planting ceased.

Massed bedding was criticised for its gaudy colours, lack of subtlety and the resulting monotony. One solution to these problems was the introduction of foliage plants. John Gibson is credited with developing subtropical gardening based on plants with dramatic foliage and unusual leaf forms, rather than on bright flowers. In Battersea Park in the 1860s Gibson planted tree-ferns, banana *Musa superba* and *Abutilon thompsonii*. These were underplanted with varieties of coleus so that the subtropical plants were shown off to advantage. Subtropical gardening added to the range of foliage plants available and provided an alternative to massed bedding plants. Many seaside resorts later found that their climate lent itself to a form of this type of planting.

Another influence on massed bedding came from the carpet system of bedding out. In carpet bedding the bed was planted with a cover, or close carpet, of dwarf foliage plants which could be kept clipped

Subtropical planting, Battersea Park, London.

Carpet bedding, Philips Park, Manchester, c.1900.

Gyllyndune Gardens, Falmouth, c.1900.

like grass or was even in texture. At Battersea Park Gibson planted dwarf grey sedum as a neutral carpet for echevaria, while in the Italian garden in Regent's Park Markham Nesfield planted panels of grass, ivy, variegated mint and other plants to contrast with vivid displays of verbena, calceolaria and pelargonium. The effect was that of a floral frieze. The advantage of the carpet-bedding system was that the plants lasted much longer than the flowering plants in the massed bedding system. In 1875 carpet beds in the shape of butterflies were planted at Crystal Palace Park and the technique was ideal for vivid horticultural displays. The technique soon fell out of favour on private estates, for such bright displays were thought to be vulgar and inappropriate for private gardens. However, it remained popular in public parks, where it received an added impetus from the introduction of sculptural planting and the floral clock. In sculptural or three-dimensional planting a wire frame provided the support for three-dimensional designs and the plants were then packed into peat or soil and held in position. Sculptural planting lent itself both to wit and to dramatic commemorative gestures. One of the most popular forms of sculptural planting was the floral clock, which was introduced in 1903 by J. McHattie, the superintendent of the Edinburgh parks. The clock mechanism was set in the ground under the bed, which was then planted as a clock face, and the hands of the clock, also planted, told the time. They became enormously popular with the public but were loathed by many parks departments. Floral clocks can still be seen in Princes Street Gardens, Edinburgh, and elsewhere.

These horticultural feats of sculptural planting and carpet bedding were much admired by the public, but they were strongly criticised by the leading private garden designers of the day. Gertrude Jekyll, who created some 350 private gardens, thought that plants should be given permanent positions and varieties should be juxtaposed so that the contrasts of colour, form and foliage were brought out at different seasons of the year. This technique of gardening was quite different from that of planting out and removing bedding plants several times a year, but it was not necessarily less expensive in upkeep. William Robinson, who advocated the introduction of the wild garden, was another vociferous critic, although he was not practically involved with public parks in Britain. Park visitors loved to see the spectacular displays of bedding plants and that was another reason why they continued to be planted in public parks.

Like many of the other aspects of parks, plants had a metaphorical as well as a practical role to play: 'Flowers not only charm, they teach.' Parks were designed not only for the visitors to enjoy but also to encourage them to become useful members of society, and the role of parks in social engineering was well understood by the park promoters. The way in which the park and the plants were maintained so perfectly and neatly would, it was thought, influence park visitors to dress neatly and behave well. They also illustrated that virtuous effort, the labour of planting and maintaining the park, gave just rewards, which could be seen in the beauty of the results. An alternative message from these horticultural displays was that the plants were cared for during their useful life and then discarded, mirroring in effect the experience of working people.

As more and more species of plants were introduced so the problem of displaying them began to occupy the attention of garden theorists and practitioners. Specialised gardens for particular plants, such as rock gardens and alpine gardens, had been established in private parks in the eighteenth century but, with the introduction of a wider range of plants and the availability of new technology, they took on a new form. Early rock gardens were usually constructed of local stone, but the Alpine Point and rockworks at Battersea Park were constructed out of artificial stone by James Pulham between 1866 and 1872. The rockworks featured streams, pools and a cascade that could be heard from afar and the slopes of the alpine garden were planted in zones of vegetation, as a miniature version of what

Peasholm Park, Scarborough: Japanese garden, c.1936.

would occur naturally. James Pulham's father had been involved in the manufacture of Portland cement and his son began experimenting in using concrete to construct artificial rockeries in the 1840s. Cement was poured over clinker, or mixtures of brick and stone, and moulded so as to resemble boulders. Pulham's works included many private commissions such as rockeries at Sandringham and what is now Bristol Botanic Garden, as well as the landscaping of rockeries in glasshouses. In Brighton Aquarium (1872) he built a fairy cave, waterfalls and a fernery, while at Rayne Thatch, across the road from Bristol Botanic Garden, he constructed an almost complete garden of Pulhamite, with a grotto, waterfalls and pools linked by bridges and stepping stones.

Among the new forms of garden introduced in the later nineteenth century were the Japanese garden and the Shakespeare garden. Interest in Japanese culture had grown since 1853, when Japan had been forcibly opened to western trade. At the 1873 Vienna Exhibition a miniature Japanese garden and village had been displayed and this was subsequently reassembled in Alexandra Palace Park, London. By the early twentieth century the popularity of the Japanese style began to be reflected in public parks and Japanese gardens were

West Park, Wolverhampton: sculptural planting for the coronation of George V in 1911.

The terrace, Heaton Park, Newcastle upon Tyne, c.1900.

THE TERRACE, HEATON PARK, NEWCASTLE.

Floral clock in Princes Street, Edinburgh, c.1900.

Prince's Parade, Bridlington: floral staircase, c.1900.

introduced into Battersea Park and Abbey Park, Leicester. One new park, Peasholm Park, Scarborough, designed between 1912 and 1929 by the borough engineer, Harry W. Smith, was completely in the Japanese style. The European version of the Japanese garden included rocks, water and features familiar from willow-pattern china. In Peasholm Park a red and yellow Japanese-style screen invited visitors to cross the adjacent Japanese-style bridge and enter the Orient. In the park was a lake with an island in it. On top of the hill on the island was a pagoda, installed in 1929, and alongside it a rocky cascade of water fell to the lake below. Beside the lake was a low pavilion and on the lake was a floating bandstand with fretted, upturned corners which continued the Japanese theme. This was further enhanced by the many lanterns which hung from slanting poles by the shore of the lake. The boating lake, putting green, miniature golf and children's model yachting pool also reflected the Japanese style. In the early 1990s construction started on a new Japanese walled garden, next to the pagoda at the top of the island.

Japanese gardens were a new type of garden planted with appropriate plants and they helped to spread understanding of Japanese plants and planting. By contrast the emphasis of the Shakespeare garden was on the plants of the past and particularly those mentioned in Shakespeare's plays. This vernacular revival was the counterpart to the vernacular revival taking place in architecture and it had been stimulated by the publication of a number of books on Shakespeare's flowers. The Shakespeare garden was introduced into public parks in London by J. J. Sexby, the first officer of the London County Council Parks Department. These gardens became very popular and also became known as Sexby gardens. The first was introduced at Brockwell Park in 1892 and the last to be created was the Ada Salter Garden (1936) in Southwark Park.

Plants and pollution

In the nineteenth century parks in the industrial cities were seen as the lungs of the city where the air was fresh, but how fresh it was depended on local industry and the direction of the prevailing wind. In Philips Park, Manchester, in the 1870s and 1880s there was so much smoke that 'the atmosphere was perfectly clouded by it and the smell of smoke was stifling'. Trees suffered most. 'The sun is obscured by rain or smoke clouds and every object is thickly clouded with the solid matters showering from the atmosphere' and it was impossible to grow pine trees successfully within 3 miles

(5 km) of the town hall. Normally trees provide the main structure to planting, but in Philips Park, the worst affected of the Manchester parks, they survived very few years. In the 1920s the amount of new planting needed to maintain Philips Park in a reasonable condition was enormous and 2500 rhododendron bushes, 2500 poplars, 1000 willows, 750 elders and 300 different kinds of flowering shrub were planted anew each year. Even then the rhododendrons flowered well only in their first year. In such a climate the planting of large numbers of bedding plants entailed far less cost and less physical effort than replacing large numbers of trees and shrubs annually.

Parks still have a role to play in moderating the climate of our polluted cities, for trees filter dust and help to clean the air and parks help to lower the temperature of the urban environment. The ecology movement and the importance of nature conservation and sustainable development are increasingly recognised and parks can play a role in the creation of green chains and green links in our cities. The creation of areas of unmown grass for wildlife had been seen both as a response to the wildlife lobby and a means of saving the expense of regular mowing. However, such areas do need close management and are not necessarily cheaper to maintain. Parks can provide wildlife habitats for certain species, but wildlife enhancement could conflict with the management of historic parks. If, for example, the demands of wildlife call for the planting of native species of trees, instead of exotic specimen trees, this could alter and damage the landscaping of a historic park. A wide variety of planting and types of garden and landscape were part of a park's attractions, but this historic landscape can easily be destroyed by the insensitive planting of trees in the wrong place, or by planting the wrong species, and by insensitivity to sight lines. In Birkenhead Park the vistas which were an important part of the design have been obscured by the insensitive planting of trees in the wrong place and in a manner out of keeping with the original tree planting in the park.

Many Victorian and twentieth-century parks featured shrubberies, which provided varied foliage throughout the year, particularly in winter. They had an important role to play in providing the structure to a park and shelter belts for the areas that they enclosed. In the 1990s, however, they began increasingly to be seen as threatening places where people of antisocial intent could lurk. As a result some local authorities introduced a policy of eliminating shrubberies or of replacing them with low shrubs.

The planting of bedding is very labour-intensive and by the early

Pulhamite rockwork in Battersea Park, c.1900

Grove Park, Weston-super-Mare: carpet bed, 1906.

Queen's Park, Longton: shrubbery showing the varied colours and textures of the different shrubs.

1990s many local authorities found they could no longer afford the costs. Where planting was still a feature, theft became an increasing problem. On the positive side, some of these magnificent carpet-bedding displays were being reinstated in the mid 1990s: for example, in Victoria Park, Glasgow, and in the Avenue at Regent's Park, London, where Nesfield's planting plan has been restored. The tradition of sculptural planting is still maintained in Morayshire in Scotland and this is one of the few places that has published a public park trail – Moray Floral Trail. Gardening is the chief recreation for 44 per cent of the population and people delight in visiting the gardens of country houses, but only a few public parks are visited in this way by garden lovers. Roundhay Park, Leeds, is one of the few public parks that attract a large number of visitors: each year over one million visit the Tropical World which has been created in the park's greenhouses.

People's parks

Parks were created as places where people could enjoy the open air and the beauty of the flowers and trees and in the process be improved socially, physically and morally. In comparison with the pleasure gardens, the activities offered tended to be rather sober and restrained, except on special occasions such as the opening of a new park or a gala. Huge numbers of people used the parks. When Blondin, the tightrope walker and hero of Niagara Falls, performed at Queen's Park, Longton, some 33,000 people came to see him. These figures were more than matched by park use in Glasgow on ordinary Sundays. When in 1883 Glasgow took a census of park use 100,000 people were recorded entering Glasgow Green on a July Sunday and 48,000 people entering Kelvingrove Park. There were similar numbers on other days of rest.

From the beginning parks provided for both active and passive recreations and what visitors were allowed to do depended on the local byelaws. The open areas of grass could be used for sports, for grazing sheep, for haymaking, picnics or meetings, but not for all these activities simultaneously. Most people could visit parks only when they were not working, on Sunday, their day of rest, but in the nineteenth century many parks were closed for part of Sunday in order to encourage people to go to church, and no games were allowed on Sundays. Religious and political meetings were part of urban life, but as parks were seen as peaceful places such potentially divisive activities were generally forbidden. There were, however, exceptions. Victoria Park in London acquired a reputation for public debate and William Morris and George Bernard Shaw were among the well-known figures who spoke there. Meetings were held on Glasgow Green and welcomed as a safety valve by the authorities. The byelaws governing the activities permitted in parks varied from authority to authority. In the Manchester and Salford parks sites were set aside for skipping, which was a popular activity for both adults and children. However, skipping was forbidden in Victoria Park, London.

The lakes could be used for fishing, swimming, boating, skating or dog-washing and again it was the local authority which determined how they should be used. In Birkenhead Park skating was allowed, but not boating or swimming. Shooting was allowed in the park in the early morning, but only of rabbits. Nevertheless, the park police were encouraged to shoot wild duck and send them in turn to members of the Parks Committee! In Alexandra Park, Hastings, the ducks

Tropical World, Roundhay Park, Leeds.

Playground with giant stride in Victoria Park, London, c.1900.

and geese had become so numerous that in 1871 two were sent to each member of the Committee. Swimming served as a way of keeping clean and in areas which lacked bath-houses men used the local canals, rivers and lakes. In Victoria Park, London, bathing was allowed in the eastern lake at specified times. Men nevertheless plunged into the water before the appointed time and when the police 'attempt to take possession of their clothes, as a means of securing their persons, the garments are carried off ... and the bather is next seen running about in a state of nudity'. While the police were thus occupied, others would also start bathing in the lake.

Playgrounds for children were included in public parks from the beginning but the Manchester Parks Committee in the 1840s found that if boys and girls shared the facilities the boys monopolised the equipment and never let the girls have a turn. Their solution was to provide the girls with their own space, with separate swings for the boys and the girls. This segregation was prompted purely by noting what happened in practice and not by any moral motives. One of the favourite items of equipment was the giant stride, which consisted of a pole with an iron top and a revolving iron cap to which hooks with ropes were attached. The ropes were either knotted to improve the grip or there was a cross stick to hold on to while running and leaping with 'giant strides' around the pole. Towards the end of the nineteenth century facilities for children increased with the introduction of sandpits, deer pens, aviaries, rabbits and guinea-pigs. At the other end of the age range some parks offered facilities for retired men to play chess or draughts and to meet all year round in heated pavilions.

The early public parks such as Birkenhead Park featured carriage drives around the edge of the park. When horses were replaced by motor cars it was decided that these had no place in parks. Some local authorities, however, recognised that parks could provide a place where children could learn road sense and Pittencrieff Park in Dunfermline included such an area in 1951. Other parks such as Lordship Recreation Ground in Haringey, London, provided a model traffic area for children to practice driving their model cars. A few parks also contained model railway lines. One was installed in Abbey Park, Leicester, in 1949 by the Leicester Society of Model Engineers. It was not intended for carrying passengers but for model railway enthusiasts.

Sports
During the last decades of the nineteenth century and in the twentieth century the emphasis on active sports increased and this had an impact on the design of parks. One approach to accommodating sports was to provide an open space in the centre of the park for cricket and football and to position the other activities around the periphery. This was Joshua Major's approach in the Manchester and Salford parks. A more pragmatic approach was to add sports facilities piecemeal as they were demanded or to separate the sports and pleasure grounds completely. As the demand for sports increased, the problem of enclosing large spaces for numbers of football pitches or cricket grounds proved impossible to solve. By 1898 Victoria Park in London had thirty-seven cricket pitches and the result was prairie-like spaces that were too large to be enclosed by planting. The range of sports offered was increasing and Battersea Park offered, according to the season, cricket, football, skating, tennis, riding, gymnasia, quoits, bowling and cycling. By the end of the nineteenth century sports for women included tennis, hockey, golf and cycling and Battersea Park became the fashionable venue for the last of these. Active sport was an important part of the movement for female emancipation, for middle-class women had not been considered strong enough for sport. Working-class women, however, were assumed to be quite able to work a six-day

Cycling in Battersea Park, c.1900.

week, run a home and bring up their children. Participation in sport challenged the view that women were passive and helped to undermine the constraints which had prevented them taking control of their lives.

During the twentieth century some parks had purpose-built sports facilities introduced into them. The National Sports Centre in London, for example, is located in the centre of Crystal Palace Park and plans for the restoration of this most important historic park have to take this into account. Although the terraces have decayed since the Crystal Palace burnt down they nevertheless still provide a venue for large-scale public events such as pop concerts and firework displays. The park was always intended by Paxton for the entertainment of large numbers of people and future plans will take this into account.

Recent surveys of park use indicate that sports players represent a very small proportion of the total number of park users and that what people enjoy in their parks is the freedom to do as they like. The voice of the sports lobby is very strong and indeed parks appear to be logical places for sports, but today's sports require more than pitches and courts; they need indoor facilities, changing rooms, restaurants and above all car parking. All these add up to large-scale buildings and large areas of concrete and historic parks are not the place for them. For the majority of park users sports are not high on their agenda. What most people like about parks is the ability to choose to be alone or in company, away from the pressures of the city, and to enjoy the space, the flowers, the greenery and the wildlife. Parks are still one of the few facilities offered free of charge in British cities.

Parks in the 1990s

Public parks developed in the context of an expanding population, increasing industrialisation and rapid urbanisation. They were brought into being by a variety of means in which social conscience, philanthropy, skilful entrepreneurship, political and municipal enterprise all played a part. The changing legislative framework gradually gave local authorities the powers to confront some of the major problems of urban living. Today that situation is reversed: local authority powers are becoming increasingly restricted and power more centralised. Some parks have disappeared, others have been decreased in size or have been radically altered. Although nature in the parks appeared in well-disciplined forms it is still a delight to see the large trees and the bright colourful flowers. There is no doubt that they provided and continue to provide enormous enjoyment, the space to run freely and safely or just to sit and dream. Gated and railed, these parks were literally and symbolically a world apart, oases of green in areas of brick and stone, places for contact with nature and to enjoy walking on grass or under the trees.

The opportunities for recreation today are enormous and some would argue that parks are no longer needed. Victorian parks were thought to 'improve' park visitors and help them to become more effective members of society by their design and the quality of their maintenance. They added to the attractions of seaside resorts and spas and they were well cared-for places, where people could meet, relax and enjoy their surroundings. By contrast, in the 1990s many parks have become run down, neglected and vandalised and the message that they proclaim is that no one cares, that there is no community and little order. It is not surprising that such places have become the target for yet further antisocial behaviour.

The major problems confronting historic public parks in the 1990s are lack of funding for maintenance and the immediate repair of acts of vandalism, and the lack of park-keepers to give people a feeling of security. Nothing promotes vandalism more than signs of evident neglect and only if parks are well maintained will people visit them. In a recent survey asking people what would most improve their parks three points stood out: the control of dogs and dog-mess; the reintroduction of park-keepers; and improving park maintenance. In some areas park rangers are being introduced and this is to be encouraged. People are very concerned about their local park and this becomes very evident as soon as any threat is posed. National Lottery funding is being made available for the restoration of historic parks and gardens under the Urban Parks Initiative launched by the Heritage Lottery Fund in 1996. Generally only capital projects will qualify and the problem of providing adequate funds for local authorities to maintain parks has yet to be solved.

Parks are part of society and they reflect the values of that society. Nowadays little value is placed on public service and every emphasis is given to cost-effectiveness. Parks reflect this only too clearly. Public parks are an important part of the urban enviroment, socially, physically, psychologically and historically. All the research on park use indicates that people still use them in the ways that parks have been used for generations: to meet in groups, to walk the dog, to take the children to play, to get away from it all, or to mark the passage of the various phases of life. People still like to feel the grass under their feet and they still need places where children can run and play in safety. Above all, contact with nature, trees, birdsong, beauty and quiet may be unfashionable, but many people will still battle to preserve them. The people who need parks most are the young, the old and the disadvantaged, those who do not have gardens of their own or private transport. These people cannot get to country parks and if their local park is threatened there is an immediate outcry. If the number of visitors to parks is declining, this is not because the design of the parks is at fault but because boarded-up and burnt-out buildings, bare flower beds and empty lakes make very unattractive places to visit. People want their parks the way they used to be: well-maintained, safe and peaceful places where they can enjoy the open space, flowers and trees and where they can stroll, relax or run around as they choose. And these are just the uses that parks were designed for originally.

Public parks are of enormous historic significance, as significant as the private parks and gardens of the seventeenth and eighteenth centuries. They are not museums, for they have always responded to change and the historic layers evident in them add to their significance and interest. We need to ensure that they continue to respond to change, while still retaining their historical integrity. Above all we need to involve people in their park and its history, for it is part of their history, and we need to involve children, for parks can be wonderful places and it is they who will be looking after them in the future.

Further reading

Despite the enormous number of parks created during the nineteenth and twentieth centuries, very little has been written about them. W. W. Pettigrew, the superintendent of Manchester parks, wrote a regular column for the *Gardeners' Chronicle*, but otherwise that journal concentrated on private estates, as did the rest of the gardening press.

Brason, Gill. *The Ungreen Park: the Diary of a Keeper.* Bodley Head, London, 1978.

Chadwick, G.F. *The Works of Sir Joseph Paxton, 1803-1865.* Architectural Press, London, 1961.

Chadwick, G.F. *The Park and the Town.* Architectural Press, London, 1966.

Comedia and Demos. *Park Life: Urban Parks and Social Renewal.* Comedia and Demos, London, 1995.

Conway, H. *People's Parks: the Design and Development of Victorian Parks in Britain.* Cambridge University Press, 1991.

Conway, H., and Lambert, D. *Public Prospects: Historic Urban Parks under Threat.* Garden History Society and Victorian Society, London, 1993.

Cranz, G. *The Politics of Park Design.* Massachusetts Institute of Technology, Cambridge, Massachusetts, 1982.

Elliott, B. *Victorian Gardens.* Batsford, London, 1986.

Eyres, P. (editor). 'Naumachia', *New Arcadian Journal* 57, 1995.

Geddes, P. *City Development: a Study of Parks, Gardens and Culture Institutes.* Geddes & Company, Edinburgh, 1904.

Jordan, H. 'Public Parks, 1885-1914', *Garden History* 22, I, 1994, pages 85-113.

Luttley, W. *Making Space: Protecting and Creating Open Space for Local Communities.* Open Spaces Society, Henley, 1992.

Major, J. *The Theory and Practice of Landscape Gardening.* Longman, Brown, Green & Longman, London, 1852.

Mawson, T.H. *Civic Art.* Batsford, London, 1911. (Part IV is on the design and construction of public parks.)

McCarthy, S., and Gilbert, M. *The Crystal Palace Dinosaurs.* The Crystal Palace Foundation, London, 1994.

Milner, H.E. *The Art and Practice of Landscape Gardening.* Simpkin, Marshall, London, 1890.

Pettigrew, W.W. *Municipal Parks: Layout, Management and Administration.* Journal of Park Administration, London, 1937.

Simo, M. *Loudon and the Landscape.* Yale University Press, London, 1988.

Summerson, J. *The Life and Work of John Nash, Architect.* George Allen & Unwin, London, 1980.

Parks to visit

The following represent a few of the many outstanding examples.

Ashton-under-Lyne, Stamford Park: excellent waterfalls and pools.

Belper, Riverside Gardens: a miniature gem with a chinoiserie pavilion, bandstand and rockwork.

Birkenhead, Birkenhead Park: Paxton's first municipal park.

Brighton, Preston Park: excellent rose garden and 1930s rockery.

Chester, Grosvenor Park: a good example of Kemp's work, very well maintained.

Darlington, South Park: excellent planting and original features; the unbroken tradition of Victorian parks still evident.

Dundee, Balgay Park: fine drives and walks; adjacent to outstanding necropolis; excellent views; site of Britain's only public observatory.

Glasgow, Kelvingrove Park: Stewart Memorial Fountain, fine landscaping and trees.

Glasgow, Victoria Park: fossil grove, quarry gardens and formal bedding.

Halifax, People's Park: Paxton and Milner terrace, small lakes and rockwork (being restored).

Huddersfield, Beaumont Park: features include wonderful cliffside walks.

Leeds, Roundhay Park: Tropical World.

Liverpool, Prince's Park: Paxton's first public park (in a neglected state at the time of writing).

Liverpool, Sefton Park: beautifully landscaped park by André (in a neglected state at the time of writing).

London, Crystal Palace Park, Sydenham: Paxton terraces, English landscaped garden and prehistoric animals (being restored).

London, Waterlow Park, Camden: steep undulating site, with excellent views of London to the south.

London, West Ham Park, Newham: rolling landscape, fine trees, rose garden, rockery and carpet bedding.

Newport (Gwent), Belle Vue Park: Mawson's subtle landscaping, with views of the estuary.

Paisley, Fountain Gardens: exceptional cast-iron fountain, formal layout.

Preston, Avenham Park and Miller Park: near the station; excellent bold designs by Milner.

Preston, Moor Park: the first municipal park; later designed by Milner.

Scarborough, Peasholm Park: Japanese garden and naumachias (mock naval battles) in the summer.

Walsall, Walsall Arboretum: excellent illuminations in the summer.

Index

Page numbers in italic refer to illustrations.